Finding Dimes

A Journey of Faith, Hope, and Prayer

by

Maureen McCormick McHugh

DORRANCE PUBLISHING CO., INC.
PITTSBURGH, PENNSYLVANIA 15222

Dorrance Publishing Co., Inc.
701 Smithfield Street
Pittsburgh, PA 15222
Visit our website at *www.dorrancebookstore.com*

ISBN: 978-1-4809-0673-0
eISBN: 978-1-4809-0719-5

To my

Grandparents

Kathleen

Anne

James

But Mostly to my brother Tim,

I miss you so!

In a world of greed, war, poverty, extreme conditions, and constant sadness, and when we all should be looking for signs of hope, I find it's often the little signs from our higher power we dismiss and explain away when we really should be embracing the symbolism behind each sign. There is a higher power. There is a kingdom where love is abundant and pain is nowhere to be found.

We have all witnessed together and separately the beauty of these signs. They warm your heart and they let the tears flow with joy in knowing that the people we have lost here on earth are secure in the palm of God's hand and the warmth of His love.

I enjoy the conversations with friends that lead to signs from someone who may have passed over—a symbol to those left behind that they have made it into God's kingdom. It is a sign only they would leave for people here to carry out their days until they too are called to heaven.

Just after my brother passed, I began to realize the pain of others who have lost someone close to them. Losing a sibling, no matter your age, is excruciating. I have lost friends and acquaintances in my life, but nothing had prepared me for the pain I was to bear when I lost my brother. Now, the signs I see over and over again give me peace and sometimes joyful tears in knowing they were meant for me. And I believe they were meant to be shared. These little symbols that cross my path almost daily have given me the strength I needed to get me through an incredibly painful experience.

I hope you, too, as you read further, will be inspired to look for *and* accept the little miracles in your life every day. Do not explain them away; embrace them and they will occur more and more in your life, bringing you joy and peace daily by each occurrence.

Finding Dimes

Many years ago, after a full and eventful life, my grandmother passed away at the age of ninety-eight. Just a few years prior, I lost my paternal grandfather and my maternal grandmother. So, for most of my adult life, I was blessed with a family of multiple generations.

When my grandfather (Dad's dad) and grandmother (Mom's mom) passed away, I started finding coins, nickels to be precise. I would walk out my door, and there was a nickel. I would also find nickels in my pockets, on the car seats, sidewalks, etc. Most of my purchases ended with getting change in the form of a nickel. I realized it was more than a coincidence. I was at a low point in my life. Financial struggles, growing children, injuries, illnesses, and daily life brought me to pray until my head hurt. I thought nobody was listening. Nickels were everywhere but I was blind to the signs of my grandparents' presence. I kept my nickel findings to myself in case anyone got the idea of messing with me.

For some time, I lay in bed at night, battling insomnia from the stresses in my life. Months had gone by and my body and mind had almost given out. I would go about the motions of my day. Finding little enjoyment in the things I used to do. Work was something I used to look forward to. It was now just that, work. I fought to get out of bed in the morning and often lost patience quickly with the things that really didn't make a difference. I felt so alone and yet I was surrounded by family and friends constantly. I was missing something. It took me a while to figure it out. But when I finally did, it hit me like a knock in the back of my head. I had lost my faith! I lost faith in love and friendships and questioned the purpose of my life.

But when? How did I lose it? What was the moment that took it away? These questions I asked in the darkness of my sleepless nights. I couldn't pinpoint any one moment. Life crept up and sucked the heck out of my spirituality. I promised myself that night I would get it back. I prayed to anyone who would listen, listing all the saints I could remember along with the Holy Family, people I knew who passed, and, of course, God himself. I figured I would gather all my sources. I prayed for guidance. I prayed for patience, and I prayed for "a sign" that someone was listening.

When I woke up the next day, I felt less burdened, less tired, and less pressure on my spirit. I didn't even notice how good I felt until I picked up the garbage to replace the bag and a nickel dropped to the bottom of the empty can. I knew then I was going to be fine. I knew then that someone heard my plea for help and somehow I knew that through my own self will, along with prayer, I would be able to move forward and acknowledge my angels. Acknowledge the happiness of taking out the garbage in the morning!

I started by making a short list of rules for myself. Some of them might seem harsh, but necessary to make my life, my husband's life, and my children's life the utmost important *thing.* I stopped worrying about keeping appearances up. I didn't stop caring about appearances; I just reprioritized my daily tasks! My house was always clean, just maybe not so organized. Instead of making sure I did the dishes before I left for work, I sometimes left them until I came home for lunch. It was exhilarating! I decided laundry days were better than doing laundry every day! And then I started teaching all four of my children to do their laundry on their own. That gave me five full days of no laundry! I stopped calling people who never once called me. I wished them well, health, and happiness but rid myself of the sole responsibility of keeping certain friendships. Unfortunately, I had to do the same with some family members. I love them all! I just may not like them so much. I walked my dog whenever it was warm. Those ten minutes was amazing. I and the one being I knew never judged me, a truly unconditional love. I miss him now and often still hear him around my home, my Goliath.

I stopped *offering* to pick up or drop off other people's children and waited for someone to *ask* for the favor. I found myself driving less, saving gas, or participating in very well-organized car pools. Don't get me wrong. I didn't lose compassion or courtesy for those in need. I just prioritized and rarely wavered from the new commitment to my life, for myself. I started walking with a friend and joined the local gym. I allowed myself the time I needed to take care of my physical being. That in turn allowed my mental and emotional being to begin to heal and free itself of the unnecessary burdens I allowed myself to previously accept.

As time went by, I started to indulge in various hobbies I always wanted to try. Some were more successful than others, but each was a stepping-stone in the right direction I was heading. I learned I have more talent than I gave myself credit for in some areas. But I also learned I might not want to pursue some hobbies in a few other areas.

I tried never to miss any of my children's home games. I say home games because I have four children, all very active in sports. Now, none of them ever felt left out. I made it a rule to attend only home games, unless an away game fell on a day or night when no one else had a game, which was very unlikely. I limited their sports to one sport per season per child. It was not an easy decision for them to make, but they stepped up and did the right thing for themselves, the teams they were on, and me! We all enjoyed removing a little "hectic" from our lives. We had more time at home and a little less on the field. The stress of making all the coaches happy, racing around town to get to multiple practices, and fast food dinners diminished. Dinner was served at a time when the majority of the family was going to be home. And my life settled down.

Now, I still get worked up over minor instances, but less often. I still like my house clean and orderly, but have accepted that in a family like mine the only time that'll happen is when I am alone. I would rather have fingerprints on the coffee table than be alone any day.

During this transition, I had moments of despair and I prayed. Soon after I would find a nickel. I had moments of sadness and self-pity and I prayed. I would soon find another nickel. I would have less sleepless nights but still found myself feeling guilty about my new life guidelines. So I would pray before closing my eyes and ask for serenity and the ability to find peace in my new decisions. Sometime during the next day, I would find a nickel. That's about when the knock in the back of my head I mentioned earlier hit me.

It was when I prayed the most that I found my nickels. Sometimes two or three a day at different moments. Someone was there by my side, walking with me, guiding me, and, at times, holding me up. It was such a peaceful feeling! And I knew it came directly from my prayers. The nickels were just a sign my angels were listening!

Grandma (Dad's Mom)

During the time I was growing up, our family spent most Sunday's visiting relatives or having the relatives visit us. I am very fond of those memories and mostly fond of the Sunday's at Grandma's house. It was the cold cuts. It was in particular the sliced American cheese. The smell of each slice, the feel of real cheese in your mouth as you bit into a sandwich made just for you. Sometimes, if you were lucky enough to be alone in the kitchen while Grandma prepared the food, she would sneak you a piece of whatever you were eyeing. She would hold her finger over her lips, signaling to keep it our secret. I also have a picture in my mind of the statue of Mary in her backyard off in the far corner, so as not to be disturbed by grandchildren running amok. My girlfriend calls it Mary in the clamshell. She has one almost as exactly as my grandparents once did. Anyone who has seen this statue, even once, knows what statue I am referring to.

My grandmother was a tough, disciplined woman from what I recall, but, as the years wore away, she softened. I don't remember a lot of hugs or kisses from her. She wasn't one for much physical affection. But in her eyes, you could see she had a light that glimmered when she spoke to you. And that light pierced right through you when she meant what she was saying. You knew when to move or when to move faster!

I mostly remember my grandparents in their later years, which is a shame, because, as they aged and I aged, we had little in common with each other. We didn't sit and color together anymore. The family's Sunday gatherings were long gone, and time moved quickly to the future. I did always keep in touch with them. Even after I moved from my home out on my own, I called them monthly to say hi. Both of them would be on the phone together, talking at the same time. My grandfather was eager to ask questions, and my grandmother was telling him to be quiet so she could hear me. It was a comedy routine. My grandfather would laugh this contagious chuckle, almost devious in nature, like he had a secret.

When I was in my early twenties, I went on a trip to visit my grandparents. They had moved south permanently, and it had been years since I saw them. During this trip, my grandfather and I were in the living area while my grandmother prepared lunch. He tapped the couch cushion next to him and motioned for me to come over. Then he leaned close and asked me what was wrong. He said he knew I was not myself by the look that wasn't in my eyes. "You look sad," he said. He knew before I did that there was something missing, besides the fact, he added, that most girls my age would have been anywhere else than with their grandparents' for a vacation. I thought about what he said during lunch, which for them consisted of more vitamins than sandwich. And, again, when I went to bed, I was sad. I was in a relationship and thought I was happy, but his comment made me think. I thought about all of what made me happy—work, friends, my family, and my relationship at the time. Every time I got back to the relationship topic, I stalled. I tried to reason with myself, denying *I* was the only one in the relationship. The other half of that situation was not there with me, and I was struggling to make him happy and depleting myself of the happiness I deserved from a good commitment. What a revelation! And to think my grandfather was the one to point it indirectly out. That was one of the first times in my life I made some life changes to better suit my desires.

During my time with my grandparents, I had noticed they kept novel items of rosary beads, a well-worn paperback Bible, and a statue of one of the saints they prayed to. There was no shrine by any means, just various comfort pieces of their religion left where they last used them. It was as if it was commonplace for these items to be just where they were in their everyday life, used and frequented whenever they felt necessary. I think this was when I realized that during my venture through the teen years, and now my twenties, I left behind a very important tool. This item would see me through good and bad, illness and health, tears of sadness and tears of joy, and times of despair and times of exuberance. What an idiot! Really? How could I have left behind the one thing that has never failed me? How could I have forgotten to take it along when I moved from home? How could I have lost and forgotten my faith?

When I got home, I made some simple and subtle changes in my life. So, needless to say, that relationship did not last. I attended church (not regularly), but when I felt a need to experience the closeness I feel to God when in his home, I think it's safe to say I am more spiritual than religious. But my religion is the basis for my spirituality. My visits to church are my own—sometimes for mass, sometimes to be alone and feel as one with God. I called my grandparents a few days after I got back and asked them about novenas, something someone else suggested might make me feel better. My grandmother talked to me about Saint Theresa, who now is my go-to saint, and I adore her! My grandmother mailed me up a copy of her favorite novena to Saint Theresa, and that copy is still in my jewelry box with the rest of my "valuables." I refer to and use it often.

Grandma's Passing (Dad's Mom)

The first time I found a dime, I wasn't even aware of its relevance. I can't remember exactly where I was or where I found it. But after a while, I began to notice I was finding an awful lot of dimes. And it all began shortly after the passing of my grandmother.

When my grandmother passed, there was a small service and funeral down South for her. I did not attend and regret it to this day. Instead, I went to a local church and lit a candle and said a prayer for her. I speak to her frequently in my prayers and ask her to be with me in times of trouble and illness. I ask her to be there for others I knew would be passing over soon or loved ones who passed over already.

When I started finding so many dimes in various places, I thought someone was teasing me. I had only mentioned it to a few people and inquired if they were setting me up as a joke. They insisted they were not. Why dimes now? What happened to my nickels? Okay, so maybe you figured it out before I ever did! Two nickels make a dime. I think my grandparents were being thrifty. It's much easier to find one dime than two nickels together. That took me years to figure out.

My Brother Tim

I noticed once again, as I had with the nickels, that I would find most dimes after I prayed. One of my favorite times to find my dimes was bright and early in the mornings. It set the tone for my day and convinced me that all would be well, no matter what the world was to throw at me.

In the fall of 2008, I received a call from my brother Tim. He and his family had moved to South Carolina, and it wasn't unusual for Tim to keep in touch with his monthly calls. We spoke for a few minutes, and then he told me the reason for this particular call—he had cancer. Prompted by his wife to call his brothers and sisters, he was reluctant to share his news but did so anyway. Tim fought a long and courageous battle with a disease that infuriates me of its existence. During his first two-year battle with cancer, he lost his bladder, kidney, and prostrate. He never faulted, rarely complained, and moved forward each and every time to cancer's next obstacle. I prayed for my brother and asked God to send the world a modern-day miracle. "*We all could use one,*" I pleaded. My brother's cancer was rare, and his treatments were more experimental than anything else. So, a miracle would be a great sign of what may lay beyond our world as we know it and a good advertisement for the Man upstairs.

It was during this time when I started to notice a pattern of my dime findings even more so than ever before. When my brother was diagnosed, and each day after I prayed, I began finding dimes everywhere. As with the nickels, I would find dimes two to three a day in places it seemed like they just appeared. But when I prayed for my grandmother to leave me and go be by my brother's side, I wouldn't find dimes for days, weeks, and sometimes months. Each time the severity of my brother's illness changed and I prayed, the dimes would come and go.

Now, that was another knock in the head. When the dimes would return, and I would start finding them again, I always welcomed it, not for their monetary value, of course, but for the spiritual connection it provided me with my grandmother. When the dimes returned, I would talk to her more frequently, asking her to be by Tim's side and give him the strength and faith he needed to overcome his cancer. The dimes would stop again; it was a pattern I couldn't ignore. The dimes came when I prayed. My guardian angel was listening, and I firmly believe it to be my grandmother. Finding these dimes are *my* modern-day miracles. They were not for everyone to *see*, but I embrace each one left for me. And I understand the importance of sharing these little signs of miracles with you.

The Strangest Places

Okay, so you need a bit more information (proof) of my dime story. Read on!

I told you already that I always find nickels, and now dimes, in the driveway, on car seats, and various other places, so much so that I started checking pockets for holes. But there's more, much more.

While working as a waitress, one of my daughters, Bridget, urged us to come in and have lunch at a local pizzeria. One rare occasion, when my husband and I both had time to share a lunch together, we decided to go and surprise her at work.

We ate for an hour or so, then said our good-byes and headed back to our car. In the middle of the sidewalk, I spotted a dime. I bent down to pick it up and my husband nearly flipped over my back because I stopped so suddenly. He laughed and said, "That's your grandmother." He's one of the few I shared my dime findings with. I put the dime in my bag and went about my day with a new sense of peace. Finding these dimes gave me such calm.

A few weeks later, after purchasing a car for my children, I went over the car with Bridget to show her where things were and familiarize her with the instruments. The owner we had purchased it from had the car detailed just before we picked it up, and it looked beautiful. This particular model car had the battery in the trunk, and, as we were inspecting its placement, I looked down into the battery's container and found a dime. I pulled it out, and we both had a smile on our faces. I kissed the hand that held it and blew my kiss upwards. My daughter continued checking the car out and found another dime in the front in a small nock on the dashboard. She kept both dimes in that car and never mixed them with any other coins. My daughter had accepted the dimes as signs of our special connection with our angels.

Dot's Smudging

When Dot, my sister-in-law, was to be fifty, she planned a wonderful celebration on the beach at sunset. During this event called smudging, we were all to reflect on days gone by, let go of ill feelings, cherish the love in our lives, and enjoy the moment we were all in. There were at least thirty of us on the beach that afternoon. Slowly, we all made our way through the "stations" of the smudging.

One of the stations we all went to was a small table where you would write down on a piece of paper a negative feeling or event you would like to rid yourself of, place the paper in a can, and move on to gather seven pennies for a ceremony later on. Dot had carefully counted out enough pennies for at least fifty people. She said she counted them out over and over to make sure she had enough every time another RSVP came in.

I walked over with my daughter Madison, and she took seven pennies. Then I went into the bowl for mine. As I opened my hand to count out the coins, I saw a few pennies and one dime! I started to cry and showed Madison my hand when she asked what was wrong. She, too, got tears in her eyes, and we hugged and cried with joy together. One of the other guests told us to put the dime down and take another penny. I took another penny, but that dime went into my coat pocket! My husband walked over to see why my daughter and I were embracing, and he smiled and said, "Only you would find one dime in a thousand pennies!" There are little to no words to describe the euphoria I felt at that moment. I felt the presence of a spirit within myself that lifted me higher to my faith than ever before.

Word got around to the other guests about finding this dime. And my family and I gladly shared brief stories of my findings. To all of us, it was a clear message we are all surrounded by miracles every day if we just take the time to see them, to accept them, and to share them with others. There were other signs to other guests that evening that strengthened their faith in their belief of a higher power and an everlasting life after we depart this physical world. It was a perfect celebration of life!

The Frog

While my brother was ill, I made more visits to his home down South than I normally would have. I was trying to squeeze the next thirty or so years into a brief few months. The trips grew more frequent as his cancer progressed, and I found myself finding dimes before, during, and after I was at his home. I never shared my findings until later in his illness when we talked about faith or our beliefs. His belief in my findings came easily. He had started experiencing his full spiritual potential more and more as the days came and went further into his fate. He told me more than once that without his faith and his strong belief that his death here on earth would bring him to eternal life with God, he would have nothing but darkness surrounding him every day.

I took my youngest son, Thomas, with me as much as possible on these trips. I mostly drove the twelve-hour trip to and from our homes. Thomas was a great traveling companion. He loved his visits with my brother, his Godfather and world's greatest uncle! They understood each other, and, by all my observations, are definitely cut from the same cloth. Most times when we visited, we stayed in the FROG (family room over garage). It's a large room with office space, a couple of twin beds, a couch, and dresser. It's rarely used by my brother's family and mostly used by the overnight guests who were now a constant. We stayed a few days, and I was starting to pack up for the trip home. I made a thorough search for random clothing that may have been left behind. Satisfied that I was ready to go, I said my good-byes and Thomas and I started to leave. For whatever reason, I ran up to the FROG to double-check if nothing was left behind, and there on the dresser, alone, was a beautiful dime. It wasn't there just minutes before. I picked it up and thanked God for the sign that my prayers have been heard. But before I left, I placed the dime back on the dresser leaving it as a symbol of the blessing it held in my brothers home.

I told no one about that finding; I just wanted to let it be. I felt it was between me and my grandmother now. We were two beings of other worlds coming together for the sake of my brother. We needed to recognize each other's existence and need for each other—even if by silent signs of random coins such as dimes.

Work

I had a few encounters with dime findings at work as well. "So what?" you may say. But I work in a kindergarten classroom, where money of any kind is not commonplace at all. No one knew of my dime findings there, until they started to appear. Only then did I share my story with the teacher I worked with at the time.

The first time I found a dime at work was a day easy to remember. My sister had called to tell me there was nothing more they could do for my brother as far as treatment was concerned. I broke down in the hall and cried. After gaining my composure as best as I could, I gathered my things and left for the day. I couldn't be of anyone's benefit anymore that day and went home to wallow in my self-pity. I started a novena to Saint Theresa, and each morning after that day, I said my novena faithfully. When I returned to work the next morning, I went about my usual routine and got various tasks done before the children started to arrive. As I was organizing the snack cups, I noticed something lying next to them. A dime! This finding almost made me cry all over again, and I struggled to keep it together. I kept the dime on the snack cart for the rest of the school year as a reminder of my blessings and the angel who is around me.

Towards the end of the school year, I was really having a hard time focusing on my days at work, and my need to be with my brother grew stronger. A good friend of mine walked up behind me as I was gathering materials, and she gave me a big hug and asked if I was all right. Well, I was until she hugged me! Then I lost it. I broke down once again in the hall and had to vanish somehow before I was a spectacle to the children. The teachers have a hard enough job explaining their lessons, never mind explaining why Mrs. McHugh was hysterical in the hallway. I ducked into an empty classroom and lifted my head just slight enough to see the counter I was standing in front of. There on the counter, amongst folders and dittos, was a shiny dime! *"Oh, my angel! My sweet voice of silence that comes through loud and clear with every finding! Thank you for being here with me. Thank you for giving me the strength to move ahead and be strong in my faith."*

In the spring of my brother's final year, my husband and I made a collective decision for me to take a leave of absence from work. I wanted to be available for my brother and his family on a moment's notice. I couldn't conceive anyone telling me I didn't have the time or days I needed to be with Tim should it come to that.

This was such a wonderful gift my husband gave me. It was absolute freedom to come and go to South Carolina whenever I needed to, whether for myself or for Tim's family. I took full advantage of this freedom and thank my husband for understanding the urgency of having to spend as much time with my brother's family as possible. My children were very supportive of this idea as well. Knowing fully well that financially we would have to buckle down a bit more, all four of my children accepted and supported my trips away from home, and, for the most part, "held the fort down" while I was away.

I also had to make sacrifices that weren't easy for me. I prefer my home organized and clean (very clean). My children have expressed my need for annual compulsive/stress management therapy! I had to let my OCD go. I couldn't expect everyone else to make the sacrifices I needed them to make without making a few adjustments myself.

Most of the time, on my rides home, just about the time I hit New Jersey, I would start convincing myself not to be alarmed or upset at what I might find when I got home. Dishes in the sink. Laundry undone. Shoes too numerous to count by the front door. By the time, I got to Long Island, the traffic had ticked me off so badly I could have cared less what my house looked like, and I was just happy to be home. My girls were away at school, but my two boys, Dan and Thomas, were still home with my husband and dog. So now you got a picture of what my house might have looked like each time I returned after being gone four or five days at a time. To my surprise, I never once found it to be unbearable. It's part of the stepping up my family did for me. All of my children Dan, Madison, Bridget, and Thomas have always been very dependable to me. When grownups have failed me, my children have not. I could ask them for consideration or acceptance in my times of need, and they always stepped up, sometimes not too gladly but always supportive.

Tom's Neck

During the time my brother was battling cancer, we unfortunately had another tragedy strike our family. My husband Tom had a life-altering accident while at work. He fractured his neck in several places, all contained within the upper cervical area. His seven-hour surgery left him able to get through his daily routines, but also left him with constant pain and despair. He emerged from the operating room with eight screws and two plates fusing his cervical area one through four permanently. His lack of movement and flexibility has been greatly compromised.

I reached out to Saint Theresa during his surgery and hospital stay in hopes to find comfort and a light at the end of my tunnel. I saw roses all around me, and it gave me a more positive attitude towards dealing with his situation. He was not permitted flowers in the ICU during his stay, but Saint Theresa has never ceased to amaze me in the comfort she brings and her roses that appear.

I traveled once or twice a day from Long Island to Manhattan to see Tom, depending on my schedule and the kids' routines. The hospital wasn't in the best of areas, but it was safe to walk to and from the parking garage a few blocks away. On the first day after Tom's surgery, I got to the hospital early. I left my car with the attendant and started to walk out of the parking garage. I dropped my keys—I only leave the car key when I valet—trying to put them into my bag. I bent down to retrieve them, and right beside the keys was a dime. I am pretty sure I laughed out loud and picked both my keys and the dime up and continued into the hospital. I told my husband what just happened and how now I was convinced my grandmother was hanging around with Saint Theresa. After all, my grandmother was the one who introduced me to Saint Theresa in the first place.

I found several dimes in the course of my husband's hospital stay, either on the sidewalk, when I walked to and from the hospital, or on the elevator floor and in the hall just outside the ICU desk. The hospital and its staff were wonderful, but the dimes were a little reassurance that we would get through this horrible ordeal.

College Volleyball

Both my daughters played college volleyball, and both did well. On one occasion, when as a family we went up to see my daughter play, I felt the need to rest. I told my husband I was going out for a nap in the car, and I moved the car to the far side of the parking lot so I wouldn't be disturbed.

I settled in the backseat and enjoyed the quiet of country life, and then I slowly drifted into sleep. Ten minutes later, I was abruptly awoken by bus of athletes just arriving. I once again got out of the car to move it further back in the parking lot. When I got out of the back door, I found a dime on the tar lot. As usual, I chuckled and put it in the console and let the frustration of being woken up wash away.

I moved the car one more time to the farthest corner I could find and turned the key to off. Once again, I got out of the car to retreat to the backseat, and, just before I sat down, I noticed another dime next to the same door on the tar lot. Only this time, when I bent down to pick it up, I held it in my hand until I drifted off to another nap. I slept for about an hour before my husband woke me for the next set of matches.

During the last few months of my brother's life, I reached out to a few people in my family whom I knew wanted to visit with him, but didn't necessarily have the ways of getting down South to do so. On one of my road trips, I invited my mother to join me. From start to finish, I found five dimes from the time I picked her up at her home in her driveway, at a rest stop—both coming and going—and at one of the hotel rooms where we stayed.

With each found dime, I just took it and tucked it into my purse and kept the joy of finding them to myself. It was my secret connection to another spiritual place. It gave me a sense of security during the trips. I really felt I had an angel with me all the time, and I rarely spoke of it to anyone, because, like I said before, I didn't want anyone messing with me—poking fun at the one thing getting me through some hard times. I didn't want it to be explained away by anyone. And, mostly, I didn't want anyone throwing down dimes on purpose just to have a laugh at my expense.

After I returned from the trip with my mom, I made arrangements with one of my sisters to go back down in a few more weeks. I drove to her home, three hours southwest of my own home. We packed up the car and decided not to wait until morning to go. Instead, we got on the road and tucked a few more hours behind us. We set a destination in Virginia and got underway.

Just before we got to the highway, we stopped for snacks and "refreshments" for later at the hotel. We also picked up a bottle of wine for our sleepover. When we emerged from the store, my sister asked if she was going to drive first. I mulled it over and said I was good for a bit and she could take the later shift. We crossed each other to get into my car, and she opened the passenger door, glancing down as she did so. Then she bent down and said to me, "Look what I just found? I just found two dimes next to each other on the ground."

I couldn't believe it. I got so excited. To me it was sign. Two dimes and two sisters on the road to see their terminally ill brother. Neither one of us was really sure who was going to drive or not. I mulled it over, changing my mind and deciding to take the first shift. Were those dimes for me alone? Yes, if I got into the passenger side. But because I didn't and my sister found them and shared her findings with me, it opened a window of conversation for us to have a very spiritual talk. She, too, found it unusual that there were two (not one) dimes together.

I felt bad for my sister after that, because we had five hours to Virginia and she heard every dime story in this book and more for the entire five hours we drove. I think her ears were bleeding when we arrived at the hotel. She was one of the few I had now confided in about my dimes. I told her about our grandmother and how I felt her around me a lot in the past years. She shared some experiences with me, and we both agreed those two dimes were a sign to us that we had an extra passenger traveling with us that trip.

On this particular trip, I had a desire to work or—maybe a better word—contribute to Tim's checklist and mark off some of the things he wanted to do around the house but no longer could. While stepping out of the shower, I looked around the kids' bathroom and saw the need to add color to perk it up a bit. So I went down to ask if that would be okay with Tim and his wife Kim, and they were all for it. I dabble in the art of faux finishes and I find it to be a comforting and calming hobby.

I decided on a color palette and technique and headed off to gather my supplies. I enlisted my sister Dianne's help, and we finished the job in a mere two hours. We dressed the room and admired a job well done. My brother Tim hadn't been upstairs in over a year because of the risk of falling and the painful task of climbing stairs. This day, he decided to make the climb and see it firsthand. He loved the finished result and admitted he only had one problem now. With a chuckle, we asked how he was going to get back downstairs. My sister, being a bit of a comic, implied I should walk ahead of him as I was the one with the most padding. We all laughed, and, yes, I did go in front of him.

Loving the bathroom outcome, Kim became eager to continue some projects on the first floor. So the next morning, I was teaching Kim a technique for a wall in her living room and then Dianne helped her touch it off with a group of picture frames she wanted to put up. We rearranged the dining room and hung some artwork. Together, the three of us were happy with the results. When Tim emerged from his bed hours later, he, too, was pleased with the work we did. He told me he and Kim always knew what to buy, but never knew how to work it into something that would make the house look like a home. He said we helped make it look like a home, and he was so appreciative of that. I was so touched he expressed that appreciation to me, and I felt like I gave him a bit more peace of mind in his battle to complete his list before he left us. His house was always beautiful but these subtle changes made his heart fill with joy.

Unfortunately, for my sister, that was the last time she would see our brother alive. But fortunately, for both of us, the trip we took was joyful in conversation, as well as our company with him. We talked about easy, light subjects and expressed feelings towards each other. We watched a movie together and even got some house painting done.

I remember clearly leaning over to kiss him good-bye, saying, "Love you, brother," and his reply of, "Love you, sister." I will never forget him calling me that because he often took my nickname and tacked on different endings in jest, and then said, "Love you, too," but never referred to me as "sister." That was the first and last time he did so. It was so funny to me that a little word like that could bring me such incredible happiness—"sister."

Home Again

After each visit to my brother's home, I had days of household chores to catch up on, and laundry had been a priority. Everyone has found change in their laundry, maybe even a bill or two. But it seems that after my last visit down South with my sister, I have found two dimes together time and time again.

My laundry, done separately from my husband's, never has coins in it. Mostly because I never carry change in my pockets, and everything is thrown into my pocketbook. But two loads of laundry in a row of my clothing, and both loads had two dimes in the bottom of the washing machine basin when I went to transfer the clothing into the dryer. The first two dimes I left on top of the dryer and smiled at finding them. I even sent a message to my sister of my laundry happening. The second load, after finding two more dimes, I took a double take to make sure I didn't drop the first two back into the washer. No. Now I had four dimes.

For most people, this would be a bit creepy. I just keep telling myself the angels around me are multiplying. And just in time, I was eager to get back down to see Tim again and always felt I would see him once more in good spirits and still with the ability to converse. I had to wait my turn, as others were filing in for their chance for a visit; his house was always filled with visitors. I was hogging every minute I could afford to go, and there were others who deserved their private time with my brother as well.

My Brother's Decline

The call of my brother's quick decline came as a shock to me. I couldn't believe my ears, and I couldn't believe I wasn't going to have that one more visit I was always so sure I would have. I have heard about it, but never experienced it before, people were talking, but I couldn't understand a word they were saying. Voices were mumbled and incoherent, the room was spinning and I felt the walls closing in on me and my world.

Immediately, plans were implemented to get down to see Tim and to assess the situation. My dad and brother Bobby went down first, and we all waited for their word on how "bad" it was. My brother Mike was there on a visit already and was holding down the home front so my sister-in-law could be with Tim around the clock. That was a Sunday.

Racing Back

By Sunday evening, flight arrangements were made, and plans for the rest of us were on hold. I picked up my dad at 5:00 AM Monday morning and drove him over to my brother Bobby's home to carpool over to the airport.

After I got back to my home, I started to pack. I packed like I was moving. I readied the suits, ties, and shirts my boys and husband would need for the funeral. I called aunts and uncles (on my husband's side of the family) and enlisted their help in coordinating my girls' traveling arrangements from their colleges to South Carolina. I called off all appointments for the next few weeks, got the car an oil change, and gassed it up. By dinnertime, everything was ready to "rock and roll," and I settled in for a restless night before I started my drive down to say good-bye one final time to my brother Tim. I became his sister again and left the title of mother and wife behind me as the miles passed by. Nothing else mattered. Nothing was important anymore. My only hope was that I made it in time while he was still able to hear me and know I was there to hold his hand and walk him to heaven.

I arrived at Tim's home around eleven on Tuesday night. My brother Mike was up waiting for me, and we spoke briefly about what had gone on during the day and then settled down for some well-deserved sleep.

Up early and ready to head over to hospice, I followed Mike to where other family members had gathered. The hospice was set in a quiet area filled with beautiful tall pine trees and early blooms of the South Carolina spring. I liked it immediately and found peace *and* anxiety as I walked towards my brother's door.

Even after all the years Tim battled this disease and after all I thought I may be prepared for, there was nothing to prepare me for the inevitable loss of someone I loved so much. At first sight, he looked so small and helpless. He drifted in and out of consciousness, and when he was aware, he was in unbearable pain. He heard everything we talked about even when we thought he was sleeping, so much so that when we talked about things he had an opinion on, he shared it. Out of the blue, he would just say his piece and go back to rest.

One particular time, I was alone with Tim and my dad. We each were at his side near his head. Tim suddenly became alert like he woke from a dream and was confused in an unusual way. He looked at my dad and then looked at me and asked, "What am I still doing here? I died like nine times already." I was floored! He was aware of his death, numerous deaths. Were those moments we watched him take a breath and then stop for a bit longer than normal deaths for him? His words were scrambled in my head. I finally realized this was a chance for me to find out where he had gone each time "he died." I glanced at my dad then asked Tim, "What was it like, can you tell me about it?" I wanted to make sure he was okay with his impending journey. It was a chance of a lifetime for me to speak about heaven with someone who made many brief visits before his final departure. He just looked at me like I was crazy and closed his eyes. My chance was gone.

Tim continued to come and go from aware to unaware for the next day and a half. On the night of February 14, Valentine's Day, Tim asked that we leave him alone with his wife for a while. We obliged and Tim and Kim spent their last Valentine's Day night holding hands and talking, just the two of them.

I went home to be with my niece and nephew, and my brothers Mike and Bobby stayed at the hospice, along with my dad and my mom, who had just arrived earlier that day. I wanted to be near Tim's children in case news came in the middle of the night. I didn't want them to be alone.

February 15

After a quick shower and making sure the dog was taken care of, I drove over to the hospice once again. Tim had a rough night and was on heavier medications than the day before. Still always fighting rest and his need to add to the conversation, he struggled with his words. The telltale signs of his departure were more prominent than the day before. I had to leave for a bit and gather my head together. I knew this was my brother Tim's last day with us.

My sisters Eileen and Dianne were en route and due at the hospice that afternoon. Eileen was driving up from Florida and Dianne down from Pennsylvania. I doubted they would be there in time to say good-bye but hoped they would. My sister Kathy had opted not to come down until after he passed, and Joanne, yet another sister, had flown in and out on the same day to share her love, say her good-byes and kiss her brother Tim for the last time.

Tim's pain had increased so badly that morning that the decision to anesthetize him so he could "let go" was made. His heart was strong, but his body and soul were tired. He would be given medication to help him sleep and be unaware of everything around him. We were all told that if there was anything left to be said, now was the time. Once he went under, he would not be able to hear us anymore.

If anyone wanted a moment, they got it. And then Tim slowly slept. He left us. My brother's life here on earth was done, and his life there in heaven had begun. And we sobbed. And we hugged and we sobbed even harder. I looked around the room and knew that my sister-in-law, along with her children, would never be the same. I looked at my sister, parents, and brothers and knew we would never have another chance for the eight of us to be together again. How sad to feel so broken.

We left the room after a bit, and the nurse told us we could go back in and sit with Tim after they got him cleaned up, which perplexed me because he wasn't dirty. We all made the phone calls to our families and made the arrangements needed, so our families would be accommodated when they arrived.

When the nurse announced we could go back in, we all decided we had enough time with him and we were ready to go back to Tim's home and come to terms with our loss. Mike and Bobby volunteered to get the belongings we had left in Tim's room. And that's when the most amazing thing happened.

Bobby's Story Back at Tim and Kim's

Back at my brother's home, we sat amongst ourselves and yet together. The CD player was playing my brother's favorite artist, and we all held a beverage of some type. One of Tim's much-loved things to do was to have his family (from both sides) at his home, relaxing by the pool, having a barbecue, watching football on high definition TV, or playing corn hole in the driveway. As long as people he loved were together and having a good time, Tim was happy. To him, that was a very important part of life—his family and a good time had by all.

As news of his passing spread, more and more people started to gather at his home. I was standing in the garage with my brother Bobby and my sister Dianne. Bobby started to tell us something about what he saw in my brother's room just as he was leaving it hours before. I interrupted and said, "Just don't tell me it was—"

He stopped me and said, "Wait, Moe, I want to see if the significance of what I found was valid. So, please, don't say anything until I am done." Asking me to be quiet is like asking me not to breathe.

I let Bobby continue and he began with entering Tim's room. Mike and Bobby had walked into the room to gather whatever we had left behind when Tim passed. Mike's hands were full; he was holding the door open with his back so Bobby could get by. As Bobby made one more visual pass to make sure he collected everything, he noticed something on the floor between Tim's bed and the bathroom door. In a space of about two feet, there was a dime. He thought about picking it up and then decided against it. He said to himself, *It's there for a reason.* As Bobby was retelling his story, I was looking at Dianne with tears of joy in my eyes. She, too, had tears and was smiling as much as I was. We gave each other a high five, knowing our brother Tim was safe within heaven, the Lord's care and our grandmother's arms. We were awestruck! What an amazing confirmation of what I had been witnessing the past few years!

Bobby knew the significance of his discovery as Dianne and I relayed a few more of the "dime" stories to him. I told my dad of Bobby's findings. My dad was one of the few I had recently shared my nickel and dime finding stories with. He smiled and simply said, "Really?" Bobby's story confirmed what I already knew—we are not walking this earth alone; we all have our angels. We just need to take the time to acknowledge their presence in our daily lives and accept their guidance when they offer it to us.

I was almost certain I would never find a single dime again. At this point, I was really okay with that assumption, because I would rather my grandma angel be with my brother Tim than with me. I didn't want Tim to be alone, and I now knew he wasn't.

Folly

The next morning, as we started to wake up, Kim had already gone out for coffee and had my favorite wake-up cup of java waiting for me. We sat and talked a bit. Things needed to be done. Visitors and family would be coming by all day, and she needed to make the arrangements for Tim's services. It was the day that became known as the "morning after my brother had died." I think anyone who has lost someone as close as I have can understand what I am trying to say here.

The sun had risen and a new day began, and I was asking how people went about their daily lives and news spread on another death in the celebrity world. Two well-known people had died just before and just after Tim's passing. I think my sister Joanne said it best. Tim was our celebrity and while the world mourned their passing, we mourned that of a great man, who, in our point of view, should be held as important to this world as that of the celebrities who passed along with him. He was our rock star!

As we prepared even further for Tim's services, I had noticed that his dog was shaking uncontrollably and unable to walk comfortably. Folly, his beloved family pet, was suddenly struck with something that needed veterinary attention. Kim decided to get him to the vet and her brother Brian volunteered to bring Folly there. The rest of us left to say our final good-bye to Tim.

Brian's trip to the vet was to say the least unusual. Folly seemed to be okay one minute and sick the next. After arriving at the vet, Folly's symptoms started to subside. His shaking almost stopped, and the vet diagnosed him with a mild ear infection.

Brain got Folly back into the car and drove home. When he went to let Folly out, the dog started shaking again and resisted walking up the driveway to go in the house. Brian was so confused. He once again packed up Folly and drove back to the vet. He told the vet, "Look, my sister is saying her final good-bye to her husband who has just passed away. I can't let this dog die, too. You have to do something for him."

The vet answered back, "Why didn't you say so in the first place? Folly is mourning your brother-in-law. He is very aware of his departure, and this is his way of grieving." Brian was not all that convinced that the vet knew what he was talking about. An animal knew that Tim had passed? But Brian once again left the vet's office and drove home with Folly. At the house, Brian was able to get Folly up the driveway, but the dog wanted no part going into the house. He tried to stand his ground and backpedaled when he was trying to get Folly into Tim and Kim's bedroom so the dog would not be disturbed by the guests coming back to the house after the services. It was so bizarre that Kim, still dressed for the funeral, needed to go to the vet to figure out what was wrong with Folly when she got home. When she was able to get Folly home, he resisted going into the master bedroom again, but finally lay down on his bed just inside their door. Kim lay down with the dog for a bit until Folly settled and felt the comfort of Kim's presence. It took days for Folly to start to return to normal.

Brian, who was a nonbeliever in our souls' journey after we leave our earthly lives, confessed to me he was astonished at what he witnessed with Folly. He truly had a change of mind and heart by Folly's behavior and the dog's ability to show such feelings of sadness and grief. I had to chuckle a bit at Brian, because the look on his face was that of utter revelation. He was so impressed by what he witnessed with an animal that he now believes Tim is still very present with us. Something I believed all along.

Still Now, In Short

My community recycle day is once a week. I try very hard to do my part, and our can, usually filled to the rim, is put out early for its pick up. As I removed the can from the street and bent over to pick up the lid, I noticed that under where the lid was flipped was a dime sitting in the street, waiting for me! I love finding early morning dimes!

Vacuuming and then finding dimes is very common now. I did a "spring cleaning" recently in our master bedroom, and after a thorough vacuuming, and I was rolling up the cord, I found a dime between the dresser and the bed. I think my grandma was recognizing a job well done!

Both my daughter Madison and my niece Dayna graduated from college this spring and were moving home. One lived in New Hampshire; the other in Connecticut. While *both* of them were moving their dressers to clean out their rooms, they each found a dime, smiling and thinking of the significance of their find and the end of such a great chapter in their lives. Both graduated with honors. Maybe they, too, were getting a message of a job well done!

Shortly after Tim passed, we also lost my stepmother. Her love of butterflies and the color orange was well-known. Sometime after her passing I held a yard sale. I was telling my friend of my stepmother's passing and lo and behold a patron came walking up wearing an orange butterfly tattoo on her ankle. A few moments later, an orange butterfly fluttered around our heads, and we laughed. Great, dimes and butterflies!

We repainted and put in new carpeting in my girls' room recently. I was preparing the room for the carpet installation. Pulling up and wrapping the old carpeting and bringing it out to trash. Underneath the carpet, under the heater, was one lone dime. Madison and I smiled. This, months after losing my brother, brings such joy in the simple finding of a coin. Home improvements are constant in my abode, and the dimes pop up with each one of them. Recently, we finished a walkway and dug up green army men, marbles, a whistle and other toys, and of course dimes.

My good friend, Debbie, has monarch butterflies that flutter around her and her daughter during the spring and summer. Without hesitation she will tell you that it's her mom's way of telling Debbie she's around her. Easily translated into her belief that her mom has passed over to a more bountiful and comforting place we know as heaven. A sign that our loved ones are still here with us, in their own way, but free of any pain they may have had in the physical life. Each sharing signs of their existence and their never ending love for us.

For anyone we've ever lost, whether a sibling, parent, child or spouse, there is an underlying love that transcends beyond our physical being. I truly believe that those that passed over are still here with us through the love we shared with them. The love that makes us grieve their passing or calls them back to us for one last smile, one last look or one last touch. The love that makes us sob at night or whisper their name when we pray.

There is one story I would like to relate that has nothing to do with dimes. Rather this is about music and a most blessed event. Just weeks after my brother Tim passed, my nephew baptized his daughter. I was still struggling to get through events not tearing up, so when the song "Carolina in My Mind" by James Taylor came on at the party after, you can imagine I needed to excuse myself. I walked around the parking lot for a full ten minutes trying to stop the tears and finally got them under control only to reappear at the party. As I walked into the room, "Tears in Heaven" by Eric Clapton was playing. I did a quick roundabout and left until I thought the song was over. Again, containing my emotions and regaining composure, I entered the room to "Knocking on Heaven's Door," also by Eric Clapton. I looked at my niece and said, "You've got to be kidding me."

My husband and I proceeded to the bar serving beer and wine only and ordered a gin and tonic. When the bartender said, "We're not serving that today," my husband slapped down twenty dollars and said in a joking way, "You are now. Get my wife a drink; she needs one." We relayed the story to the bartender, and he made it a double. It wounded up to a great laugh.

One specific day I woke up anxious, edgy, and overwhelmed with my list of things to get done. I started out to my mother's home to paint her extra bedroom, a task I put off long enough and needed to cross off my list. Usually, painting calms me, and I go off into another place of peace. Today, I just wanted to get it done and get home, park the car, and stay inside. When I got home, my nephew Timmy was inside the living room, enjoying a cup of coffee with my husband, my brother's son, my godson, and an all-around great kid. He hung out for a while and we got to talk about work and his future plans. I made a phone call to my sister-in-law, Pat, to see if her connections may be beneficial for him to talk to. In a family my size, we got someone working in some profession somewhere. Pat, as always, was more than happy to make some phone calls and offer advice for my nephew. We spent some time on the phone discussing about possibilities and heading in a direction of some sort. I conveyed my conversation to my nephew, and then I went outside to take a picture of my house.

The last few weeks, we had renovated our front yard, and my sister-in-law hadn't seen it yet. So, during the conversation, I mentioned to her that I would take a picture of the work and send it to her via my mobile phone.

I went to the front of the house and stepped between my kids' cars to get a full view. As I stepped off the curb, I looked down, and there were two dimes together on the asphalt just a few inches apart. I picked them up and my lip started to quiver. When I went inside, my nephew was on the phone with his mom, Kim. So, I tossed the two dimes on the table in front of him and smiled, stating, "Look what I just found!" He, too, smiled and told Kim what I just walked in with.

I took it as a sign that not only was my grandmother with me, but my brother as well, all the while thanking me for putting forth the effort to help his son out. He is here every day with each one of us. It is truly amazing—the signs he leaves, the smile it brings, and the love it shares, instantly.

I still remained anxious for the remainder of the day, and when I looked at the paper, I noticed the date. Eight months had passed since I lost my brother to heaven. Eight months had gone by like a dream, a blink of an eye. And I realize that no matter how much time passes, my tears still flow, my heart still breaks, and God I miss him so!

My all-time favorite has to be during a conversation with Kim. Wednesday's are especially hard for us. It marks an anniversary of Tim's passing. She called me while I just finished vacuuming. (Remember I like to clean!) Our conversation was, of course, how we were feeling Tim's loss and its effect on our lives. I also felt like I was going through the days with no direction; just getting through them instead of enjoying the moments passing by. I found little joy in the events that usually brought me happiness. I actually said to her, "I really need to stop and start smelling the roses again." While still on the phone with her, I was wrapping up my vacuum to put it away. I bent over to pick up the cord, and there was a dime in the middle of the floor. I just finished cleaning! Not two minutes later, the doorbell rang and a dozen roses appeared from the outstretched hands of the delivery person. They were for the condolences of my stepmother's passing. Kim and I couldn't believe it. Saint Theresa, my no-fail favorite saint. I finally hung up with Kim and stopped and smelled my roses!

And, yes! I keep finding dimes, everywhere!

As I sat in my living room, after returning to Long Island from Tim's services, I held the hand of my dear friend, Gina. We cried for each other and the pain that came with our loss—her mother, her nephew, her friends, and relatives; my brother, my relatives, and my friends. We held hands and cried, until our breath was gone and our hearts ached.

Just after Gina and I dropped hands, my husband said something from behind me. I turned to answer him, but I had to stop mid-sentence. On the wall in the room before me were the letters GOD from the sun coming through my window. I felt weak and shocked. Gina, my husband, and I were in awe. I ran for my camera, but each picture I took came back with a black background and hard to read. This was at four o'clock in the afternoon, and my house was bright with sunshine. I now have a dark picture I kept to remind me of what had happened.

To be honest, I tried hard to see the letters whenever I could, but I never had again. My husband stated he had never seen that before and we have lived in this house for nearly seventeen years. When Gina shared this event with someone, they explained it away. Instead of embracing the sign that God's presence was there with us just when we needed Him most that day, they said, "The glass was beveled and threw the light off."

Embrace the signs of a wonderful world yet to be known to us. Keep it to yourself or share your experiences with a friend. Nevertheless, enjoy these signs and symbols because they are meant for you. They are meant to make your heart flutter and your lips smile. But I think, most of all, they are there to give us hope that one day, we, too, will be in a better place, sharing signs with those we have left behind.

Walk You to Heaven

I want to walk you to heaven
And make sure you get there safe
Protect you like a little boy
When you're greeted at the gate
I want to walk you to heaven
And have a talk with God
I need to know some answers
That I know I'll take real hard
I want to walk you to heaven
To have a chance to explain
You really need to stay with us
For our lives won't be the same
I want to walk you to heaven
I'll scream and kick and cry
Maybe God will change his mind
And won't make me say good-bye
I want to walk you to heaven
But I know this can't come true
'Cause if I walk you to heaven
I'd want to stay there, too!
I love you, brother!

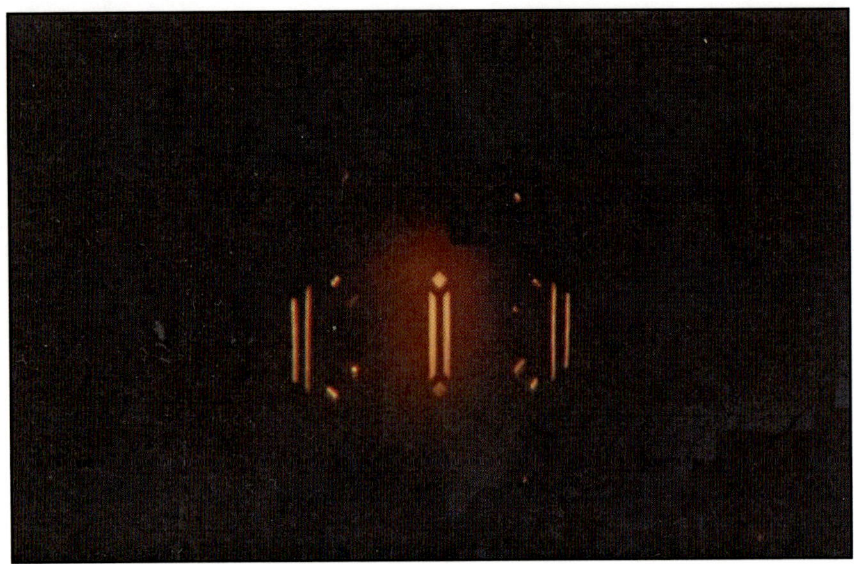

The letters GOD as they appeared while sitting with a friend.

Saving pictures to my computer, the letters GOD, again, appear before I got a chance to name the file. The pictures were of my brother's daughter's graduation in South Carolina.